AF574664

WALES
in our own
IMAGE

Preface by Jan Morris

WALES
in our own
IMAGE

Published for Millennium Wales by IN BOOKS
First edition published May 1999

ISBN 0 9535303 0 2

Designed, typeset and printed in Wales

PO Box 105, Cardiff CF14 5YB, Wales, UK

Looking forward

Preface

In the history of every people there are moments of new start and high hope, all too often achieved by violence but sometimes by evolution. It is an evolutionary festivity that is symbolised by this book. At the very end of the 20th century, after 800 years of political impotence, the small peninsular nation of Wales, in the western flank of England, has won for itself a first degree of democratic self-government; and it has done so not by bloodshed but by patient argument, stubborn example and persuasion – gradually, and on the whole without lasting bitterness. It is a true cause for national rejoicing, and for a touch of national swank, and this happy volume is an expression of both.

The *leit-motif* of the celebration has to be reconciliation – reconciliation with outsiders, but also reconciliation with ourselves. For centuries Wales was hardly more than a congeries of squabbling tribes, now and then forced into a reluctant unity by one charismatic prince or another. Even in our own times there has been an allegorical gulf between north and south, encouraged and exaggerated indeed by snide observers from over the border, but still real enough. And until only yesterday there were rumbling jealousies and dissensions between those who spoke the Welsh language, and consequently often thought themselves inherently more Welsh, and those who did not, and so tended to believe themselves essentially more worldly. These very divisions, of course, helped to keep the nation in its condition of historical subjection, and it is part of today's exultatory mood, part of the character of this book, that with luck we have now seen the worst of them, and can look forward to a new Wales that is friendlier to itself.

Harmony between past and present is a second theme of the moment. For years Wales has too often seemed sunk in the debilitating abstraction known to publicists and developers as 'heritage' – castles, folk-traditions, half-timbering, quaint costumes and all that. If there is one country that need not be trapped in this tinsel trap, it is Wales, because here as vividly as anywhere old things and new easily and sometimes comically overlap. A castle stands unselfconsciously next to a garage or a supermarket. A medieval kind of troubadour doubles as a rock singer. The relics of the dead coal industry seem as movingly archeological as the crypt of a Norman church. The Welsh landmass itself, bony and craggy and brown, is as well-designed for motorbike scrambles as it is for monkly processions, and the devices of Welsh-language poetry are used today exactly as they were in the 14th century. Now, at the start of a new millennium, Wales is realising that there is no need to belabour its past, which is always with us anyway – only a duty to respect and cherish it.

At times of revived national identity it must always be a temptation somehow to impose logical patterns upon countries. Wales is so small, as countries go – only 150 miles from north to south, never more than 100 miles from east to west – that any self-respecting despot could easily discipline it into uniformity. Fortunately, there are no despots around at the moment, and the Welsh character is fundamentally anarchic, or at least argumentative – two Welsh people, it is often said, make a debating society. The deadening forces of our age, of course, have dulled many Welsh edges as they have dulled edges everywhere, but still this remains a country of inexhaustible variety. Its people are varied, its landscapes are varied, its involvement in all the arts is eclectic and often eccentric, and it packs into its 8,000 square miles an almost gaudy range of spectacle and allusion.

Gaudiness may not be apparent to the visitor, God knows, who stands for the first time on a deserted Welsh railway platform waiting for a train, while the drizzle spatters on the station roof and a solitary drop-out snores flat on his back on the waiting-room bench. It is, though, embottled (if there is such a word) in these pages. Wales is a duplicitous country, revealing deeper truths about itself mostly in glimpse and nuance, but its colour and vivacity is always latent there, even beyond the station yard on a wet Sunday evening. It has always been sporadically apparent at pubs and *eisteddfodau* and rugby fields, on the stage and at the rock concert, but as a national exception, rather than the rule: now it is time, at last, to proclaim it the Welsh norm.

In fact what this book is proclaiming is the future. Even in old Wales, after all, the future is the norm, and like a chrysalis it is emerging from the past and present to blossom (we hope) into new energy and pride. The poets and authors who have written this book, the artists and photographers who have produced its marvellously variegated images, the actors and musicians and sportsmen and farmers and businessmen who figure in them – all seem to me to be looking if not always with confidence, at least with hope towards a newly revealed Wales, freed of inhibitions and reputations alike. If it seems a somewhat fractured revelation that the book presents, that is doubly proper. For one thing Wales is a pointillist kind of country, made up of a myriad tiny organisms which constitute a whole only if you know how to look at them. For another, although this is a celebration of a new Wales, to be frank we are not there yet. We need to convince the rest of the world that we are on our way: we need to convince ourselves that we can get there.

Can we? Judge for yourselves from these pages. For myself I believe that, for all the cheerfully pragmatic newness they display, still we must depend for our success upon three ancient qualities of Wales: kindness, consistency, and the faith to be true to ourselves – qualities which have sustained us through so many centuries of ignominy, and can guide us now, if we honour them properly, through generations of success. Many a contemporary Welsh poet – for Wales is above all a land of poetry – is expressing these aspirations in the idioms of our time: but here is a prophetic lyric written half a century ago by a poet of an older generation and a simpler style, John Morris-Jones, and translated into English a quarter of a century ago by another, Gwyn Williams, which reads more relevant than ever today:

... And yet I sing my country,
For Wales shall one day be
the happiest and loveliest land,
a time when we will see
no violent hand to waste her,
no coward to betray her,
no quarrelling to weaken her
and when Wales shall be free.

Jan Morris

Baton charge – Owain Arwel Hughes, Welsh Proms *(above)*

Graduation ball, Aberystwyth *(following page)*

Promising Light
for Al Jones, photographer

"Omo!" and "Daz!" they call him: mud-layered, unwashed skin. Even here he can hear the children taunting, fingers to ears at their low-flying brays.

Out of focus, in smoky mist, the skip slobbers a piece of rag and a battlefield of rubbish reveals the bones of all we consume.

He wears his medals proudly: keys dangled from his lapel, the caravan his waiting shell. He'll crawl into it like some wounded crustacean.

His hair reaches out: brown-grey bines the only bush on a decimated moor. Fagin-featured, yet he'd steal nothing, preferring to rummage among dead-ends, where Third World meets First. Outcrop of his wrinkled brow promising light the clouds deny.

Mike Jenkins

Summit meeting

Welsh landscape

The young ravens are feeding along the tousled shoreline of Menai, a full and flooding tide ripples its small waves across the sandflats of Traeth Lafan, the Carneddau are skeined with close mist and, in the gladness sight of this scene brings, I realise again how profoundly thankful I am to live in this small, jewelled country, this quiet masterpiece amongst the world's landscapes, its fine-worked canvas stretched out between Worm's Head and Holyhead.

What is it about the physical form of Wales that so enduringly appeals? There is, I suppose, an arguable aesthetic of landscape within which the physical form of Wales could be valued, and for light and grace and shading placed higher maybe than gloomy Scotland, Ireland's bungaloid west, the crowded Lakes or the dirty Peak. But the pull of this country is more visceral than that. It is foreign, other, apart, and that sense echoes through all the litanies of its hill-names with their veiled stories or clear-sighted observations: Ffordd Gam Elin, Bwlch Cerrig y Gigfran, Rhos y Gwaliau.

So in the true nature of love, we come to it not as seekers after our own reflection but for its mystery. There was an October night, yes, and by Cyfannedd a gibbous moon cast latticed shadows of branches across the road, an owl's wavering scream tore at the woods' silence, curlews descanted in the estuary. I took the footpath across the Barmouth rail-bridge with slick, black water running fast beneath, between the baulks which the shipworm gnaws, Enlli's light flashing out west, and all the while the prone, dark ridge of Cadair Idris brooding behind me and more shadows of hills in front waiting for the light of my next day's journeying.

I have so many of these memories. I travel endlessly amongst these hills which are the essential Welsh landscape and am never satiated. My home is in the Welsh mountains, and has been since I was free to make that choice. When I'm away from Wales, I find myself often longing for so simple a thing as the sage-green or the orange or the may-green lichens of a Welsh mountain or seaward slope, adorning rock the colour of quicksilver or hard and veiny as seasoned timber and clean as the wind. When I think of Wales, often I do not think of its obvious uniquenesses – its palpable sense of history and loss, the difficult harmonics of its language, its otherness – but of its more intimate detail. There are the streams to which, if you were led blindfold, ignorant and disorientated, you could never mistake for a Lakeland beck.

'Look,' say the rocks through which they bridle and thrill their way, 'we are *Welsh* rocks. Geology itself has borrowed the names of our tribes: Silurian and Ordovician. And look at the ferns, look at the flowers which adorn us. Where else would you find these riches?'

There are the arctic-alpine flowers too. I go up each Spring amongst the mountains to find them, to see what is growing, and where, and in what quantity. I go to Clogwyn Du'r Arddu high on Snowdon, perhaps, with the mist louring so that its dark, sheer faces loom above and the swirl of vapour by tricks of perspective transfers movement and gargoyle trickery to the rocks. Amongst which, out of the greyness and obscurity, suddenly you see a glimmer of colour, approach it, and there are the fleshy leaves and yellow flowers of rose-root hanging down, or the pinks and purples of saxifrages and moss campion, or the delicate white grace of the Snowdon lily, or thyme spreading, simply. And to see them there, so small and fine in such a savage place, fills you with a beneficent sense of marvels.

Or I turn from the detail of the canvas to outline and tonal range, for example: the sharp, pyramidal symmetries of Cnicht, with the falls and flow of Afon Croesor washing the foreground and the oakwoods of the valley sides densening the texture of the scene. Or any one of a dozen different perspectives on Tryfan, or the way in which the line of the crest of those hills which enclose Cwm Pennant to the north-west, and which is visible from so many locations in central and western Snowdonia, imprints itself upon my awareness and sense of the place so that the recollection – just of that outline, nothing more – cuts in with the loveliest clarity often and often in the mundane and dreary moments of living.
To bring relief and release. It is important to let these things register, to acknowledge them, and for me, it is from the landscape of Wales that all the crucial images, *'Felt in the blood, and felt along the heart,/And passing into my purer mind/With tranquil restoration',* derive. Physically, this is Britain's masterpiece. Appreciate it thus.

Jim Perrin

Adorning the rock *(above)*

Snowdonia, *Eryri* – land of eagles *(left)*

Dome – National Botanic Garden of Wales *(above)*

'...always a shock
those beings in stone disguises
the peasant's hut transformed to a palace of wonders'
from 'Sculpture at Margam' by Hilary Llewellyn-Williams *(top right)*

A remembrance of war – Cathays Park *(right)*

The high-life, St. David's hotel *(far right)*

Tower of strength – the last deep pit, bought by its workforce

Queen of rock – Cerys Matthews of Catatonia

Bird watching – ceiling at Castell Coch

Deep Song

At school, we all sang soprano
sending our voices clear
through the tops of our heads,

our new-bloom women's bodies
ethereal beneath the stiff
pleated maroon

and as the notes flew up, we rose too,
hovering on plumes of pure sound,
the shriven vowels of nuns.

But between puppyfat and agelines
I lost that voice, I lost
all angelic strivings

visible now out of that uniform
of fluting descants, visible
and fleshly, having descended

to earth, my substance.
Now when I sing the sound rises
not from my throat, but lower,

from my centre, from the ground.
I've found my true voice in the register
of trees and stones and water:

so growing up means growing down
and deeper in. I've left heaven
to the birds with their child voices

while I rework the element of earth,
stir it with blood, with an old
unholy laughter. Listen:

the held note of the earth;
its pitched drone keys
all my music. This is my sphere,

its voice my voice.
I only visit the air
in rare dreams of a childhood spent there.

Hilary Llewellyn-Williams

Pembrokeshire farmer with one of his primitive sculptures

Vertical drop *(above)*

A light shower *(left)*

Hard rock, heavy water *(previous page)*

Venetian facade – Queen Street, Cardiff (above)

An elegance of spirit – children's festival *(right)*

'This is their territory of sand,
unstable as a glacier,
where history is molten'
Robert Minhinnick

A footnote in the Book of Tides

They are here on Christmas Day. They are here in bad weather. They will be here in the dusk of millennium eve. I like these people. These people who use metal detectors. Here they are at 10 p.m. on the beach in front of the funfair. They sweep the sand where soon the waves will jostle in a muscular throng under the floodlights.

What can I call them? Searchers, seekers, fools? What is there for them on this coast but the smooth artemis, the 'bowlingo' token from one of the arcades? But they are not fools. This is their territory of sand, unstable as a glacier, where history is molten. Here the Bronze Age rubs against the age of plastic and the torque of a chieftain might lie within the wrack-tangle of high tide. These are dreamers on the beach, all of them men and all of them solitary, listening to the sand as blackbirds will listen to a lawn, patrolling the beach in a choreography of dreams. The sea is racing towards them, dark and smelling of olives. The sky is a ruin around us. I leave them to their sweeping, as serious as prayer.

Every night at the High Tide I lose money. But everyone loses money at the High Tide. That is why every night we come back to the machines that sigh and tremble as they release the sump of coins, as they stand glimmering as we pour the silver back in, some of us postulants, others irreducibly dedicated, playing three machines at once, baling out coinage, pushing it away from us, getting rid of money as if it was a curse in our lives, ignoring the victories as pennies gush back into the room, but getting rid, getting broke, getting down to the simplicities, getting purified, getting born.

My companions on the line tonight are a family. The man is red and bursting under a streetmarket CK singlet, his sunrash livid as chillipeppers. The weights machine has filled him out, but what hair he might have had has vanished after a Number One, the bristle like a smudge of newsprint. This man is bored with the machines. He's not a gambler, but the woman is besotted. A demon of the arcade shines out of her eyes, forces her right thumb against the slots. Because the man is with the woman the man plays too, passing her the plastic money bags, each one emptied in less than a minute and dropped at her feet. Occasionally he takes a swig from a foil-necked bottle and that's when I can read his tattoo. The needlework on his left bicep spells out her name. For some reason I feel it will be his epitaph.

The woman is brown. Tonight she owns the gambler's pallor, deliberate, obsessional, but her belly is dark beneath the croptop, a tiny golden serpent piercing her navel. A rush of coins rattles the shute but this woman does not vary her routine, and it is the man who gets down on his knees to gather the bounty in two huge hands, laughing at the good fortune which is already disappearing into the mouths of machines up the line.

On the steamtrain in the corner their son rides around the world. He is shorn like his father, head yellow as an apricot, a darker scalplock braided behind, the little rattail twisted with a scarlet thread. He has a star in his right ear, a transfer on his arm. His mother has fed the train in fifties and as one journey finishes, another begins, past Snowdon and the Taj Mahal, the sea against the pier wall climbing towards him every thirty seconds, a black escalator that leaves a ghost of itself behind on the breakwater. This is strange, but no stranger than the Ghost Train where he cried when the siren started and the faces crowded into the darkness that had been filled with the skin and the perfume of his mother.

An older woman stands with us, and a youth in Juventus black and white. The woman has a driftwood face, and I think of the grey, salt-cured implacability of the spars on the tideline. At home I have a room littered with the knuckles and femurs of such anonymous wood, but this High Tide denizen is made of the stuff, a drift-wood idol come to life. How quickly her careful coins are vanishing. Soon she is drifting away.

Now a cocklegirl walks through, stiffbacked with her tray of crabsticks and cones of Penclawdd gold, but the family-bars are emptying, and the final assault on the machines is mounted by the spent-out, the spent-up, the first come and the last served, and ten yards distant the sea is a pit where neon figures wave and drown. Someone throws a litterbin into the waves. Tomorrow it will be returned, though a thousand years might not make their mark within the book of tides.

Robert Minhinnick

Dunraven Bay

Hydro power, Elan Valley *(above)*

The red kite is the most beautiful bird of prey in Britain. Driven to the edge of extinction, it maintained a claw hold in the river-green gullies of Mid Wales. The story of its protection is a champagne tale of conservation. Today, this elegant swallow-tailed survivor continues to expand its range, aerobatically swooping over sheep folds and scything through big skies *(left)*

Circus school, Cardiff *(previous page)*

Oscar-nominated animation, the Canterbury Tales *(above)*

Precision movement
Diversions – Wales' premiere dance company *(top left)*

Ed Thomas, dramatist *(left)*

The Aliens

They brought a foreign warmth
To valleys bleak with strife
And Calvinism, brewing
A relaxation in the coffee cups.
And sunny voices learned
The mysteries of a tongue
Dark with the shadows of an ancient war.
They read the native ways
But kept, perhaps, an irony
Hidden behind their friendly, Latin eyes.
But they were too polite
To mock our self-denial,
And anyway, it wasn't good for business.

Their cafes, innocent
Of obvious sin, were yet
Viewed with disapproval by the folk
Who idolised a God
Who never smiled on Sunday,
And thunderously visited a curse
On all who stepped inside
To buy a box of matches for
A pipe of surreptitious Sabbath peace.
And yet the cafes spread.
And they became accepted.
And God, at last, was able to relax.

Times change. Some chapels now
Are turned to supermarkets,
The gospel is according to demand.
And hedonistic clubs
Have striptease on a Sunday,
Behind the seventh veil lies the promised land.
But still the Rabaiottis,
Bracchis and Antoniazzis
Keep their faith in God intact
And their attitude polite:
The customer, of course, is always right.

Herbert Williams

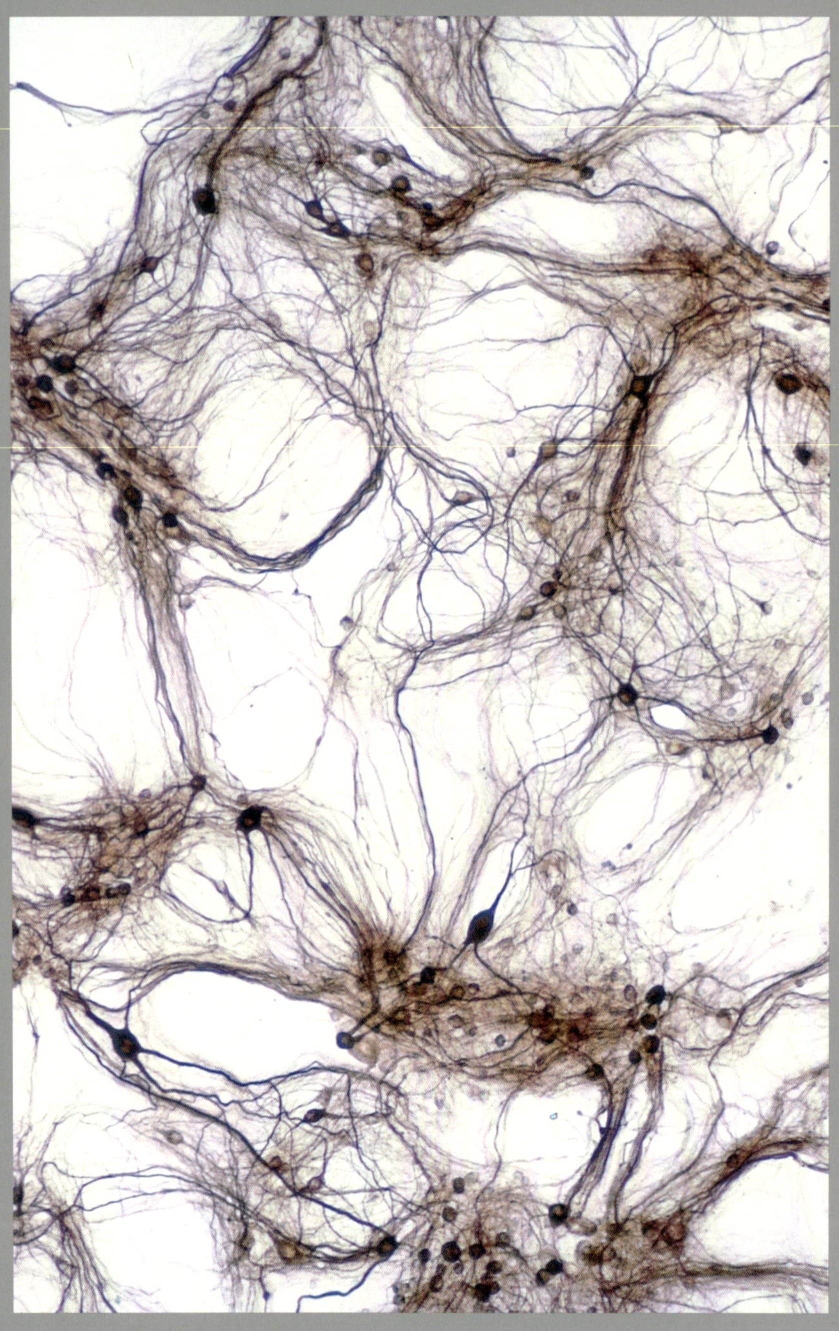

Pioneering science – 'suicide cells', created by Dr. George Foster and Brad Fisher may be one key to treating brain diseases *(above)*

Going for chips – hyperclean workplaces for tomorrow's technologies *(right)*

Swan lake *(previous page)*

Land of invention

While poets, singers and patriotic warriors are the heroes of our national anthem, the achievements of Welsh scientists and technologists, out of all proportion to the size of our population, are unsung and all but invisible. Whole fifteens of 'patriotic warriors' may be confidently recalled in rugby clubs throughout the land, but ask anyone to name just one Welsh scientist and you'll probably be told, 'a contradiction in terms, mate'.

What little science (literally, 'knowledge') we have of ourselves. Poets have been championed now and then as suitable candidates for a Nobel prize, but only one contender from Wales has actually won a Nobel, Brian Josephson from Cardiff, a scientist whose work in low temperature physics is on the threshold of revolutionising computer technology. Poetry and science might seem to inhabit mutually exclusive worlds but it is to poetry that we must look, the medieval 'nature gnomes' –

Cold bed of fish in the gloom of ice;
Stag lean, bearded reeds;
Evening brief, slant of bent wood.

(translation Tony Conran)

– for the beginnings of what has become a remarkable if unacknowledged Welsh scientific tradition. These chains of frequently three-line verses amount to a methodical investigation of natural phenomena, classifying the effects of, say, winter in terms of physics, botany and zoology.

'Of all the human activities where Wales has excelled it is in science that our contribution has been superlative', says the Aberystwyth-based space scientist Phil Williams. He cites figures such as Robert Recorde (d.1558) of Tenby who wrote the first book on algebra in English and invented the 'equals' sign (=); Alfred Wallace (1823-1913), the naturalist from Usk who beat Darwin to the discovery of the principle of 'the survival of the fittest'; Corwen-born David Hughes, inventor of the microphone and the teleprinter; Evan Williams of Sychpant, 'the most outstanding Welsh scientist of all time', who discovered the meson particle. The most important Welshman alive, he argues, indeed 'possibly the most important person in the world' is Dyserth-born John Houghton who, as chair of the scientific committee of the Intergovernmental Panel on Climate Change, is responsible for the scientific evidence for global warming. Houghton's reports led to the crucial Rio and Kyoto summits, and international agreements on the imperative of cutting carbon dioxide output.

If science, being an international pursuit, has drawn Welsh brains to institutions all over the world, it has also generated more than enough home-based activity to make a scientific career in Wales an attractive option. Wales ranks top in the United Kingdom in the amount of money spent on invention and in the successes resulting from that investment. The University of Wales, the second largest in the UK, has equipment worth £150 million and a huge fund of pioneering expertise which is available to industrial and commercial concerns.

Some of the most exciting science of contemporary Wales, and to many the most disturbing, is in DNA research and the genetics revolution. At the Institute of Grassland and Environmental Research (IGER) near Aberystwyth they are genetically modifying grasses to breed hardier, higher yielding, pest-resistant strains. At the University in Swansea they're breeding male-only tilapia fish to increase the yield of Third World fish farms. At the University's College of Medicine in Cardiff they're lighting up human cells with the bioluminescence of the firefly in order to investigate the behaviour of live cells in diseases like rheumatoid arthritis.

Wales is where the Industrial Age that shaped the modern world began, but that age and the subsequent Petrochemical Age are in historic transition to the Biotech Century, with Wales, playing a leading role. Genes are the raw resource of a new epoch in which the information and life sciences are fusing into a single powerful technological and economic force.

This transforming world, in which all that once seemed solid melts into 'For Sale' signs, presents us with great intellectual and practical problems, in addition to profound moral dilemmas. A society in which most people seem to believe in astrology and half the population thinks the sun goes around the earth is hardly fit to form an opinion on such vital matters as, say, the corporate ownership of life patents. To make the most of the possibilities and to confront the dangers, we need in Wales a new, non-acquisitive politics, an educated and informed populace, and the vision to create opportunities for ourselves, rather than hang about waiting for 'inward investors' to drop in and sort us out.

Nigel Jenkins

Horizontal hold *(above)*
Conveying delight *(left)*

Surf's up, Porthcawl *(top)*

The rocks of the world are named after ancient Welsh tribes – Silurian and Ordovician *(above)*

Brother Gildas, meeting the boat to bring visitors to the monastery on Caldey Island *(right)*

Bestiary
from 'Tone Poem'

Python-coils of leg and trunk
confuse the hand:
where do I stop and you begin?

That thumb-size hare
we saw in the Egyptian Gallery
had your stretched-back neck now

but not these fingers
grazing and ruminating
all over my back.

You bird-burr my name
then pigeon-pout oohs and ahs
as I grunt and root deeper.

Flopped apart,
flounders washed up
on the slab of the bed,

we gape at our groins
fresh-sprigged with dark parsley
and remember

how earlier that night
we kissed in a church doorway
as fire-engines whooped by

their lights flocking over us
the sudden flits and blues
of passerine and paradise.

Oliver Reynolds

Duck supreme *(above)*

Cosy café *(left)*

Divine interior, St. David's Cathedral *(previous page)*

They bought a mountain –
Sir Anthony Hopkins presided over a successful
public appeal to save Snowdon

Water bed – Aberdaron mussels *(above)*

Surge – Mewslade Bay *(left)*

The learning experience

The Welsh language

The Welsh language, *yr iaith Gymraeg* is full of hard hitting consonants *(b, c, ch, d, dd, f, ff, g, ng, h, l, ll, m, n, p, ph, r, rh, s, t, th)* and soft lulled vowels *(a, e, i, o, u, w, y)*. It might seem to the outsider the language of the deranged. Yet this intricate and ferocious language has been thick on the tongues of the Welsh people for centuries. We like a good boast, just like the tale of Taliesin. We boast the longevity of the language, its vibrancy and its resilience. And though we're good in Welsh on names we're not so good on numbers. We only whisper the fact that only half a million speak it.

St Patrick used it to swear – in the fifth century. Aneirin a century later used it to relate the battle of Catraeth (Catterick) and name each and every one of the three hundred lost but kept alive in verse. Dafydd ap Gwilym used it to entertain us with comic tales of love and misadventure in the Middle Ages. Whatever its purpose, the language has been through the mill. The language which was once condemned on the board of the 'Welsh Not' a century or so ago is now in the hands of another type of board. The Welsh Language Board. Yes, the language of civil disobedience has become the language of the civil servants.

Everyone in Wales has an attitude towards Welsh. It is one of the most notable features of our existence. In fact, while Ireland and Scotland held on to their history but for a time slackened the grip on their languages, the history of Wales was always bound up with the language, whether it was the translation of the Bible, the Treason of the Blue Books or the Snowdrops of Temperance. Bible Welsh versus pub Welsh. Even the horses following the 1904 Revival would not move because they had only ever heard expletives. The sobering of the language made them too soberly in fashion.

Today, Welsh moves in a multitude of ways. It can mumble, grumble or gabble or be eloquent. We can cringe and whinge in Welsh. And sometimes even mutate. Nasal, aspirate or soft. They are necessary, especially with the sticklers. But the language is even more diverse than those who speak it and there will always be those who delight in the language without being able to utter a word. Identity, it seems, transcends language.

Nevertheless, in the 'nineties, the language has matured. It has grown up in new surroundings. It's become for some a profession. In the 'seventies the unexpected demand to be heard in court in Welsh would result in such comical moments as the announcement by an inept translator of a *croeshoelio* (crucifixion) instead of *croesholi* (cross-examination). Welsh-language protesters sitting in the middle of Oxford Street, London would often be arrested by bemused but friendly Welsh-speaking policemen. We tend to forget the 400,000 speakers outside our country who yearn for their roots.

Today there is a growing awareness of a sophisticated bilingualism and its horizons are recognised within a multilingual Europe. The Innuit always pride themselves in their numerous words for snow and the Welsh language too is beholder of thirty words for love, struggle and survival. We have two words for know – *gwybod* and *adnabod* – which suggests deeper understanding, from knowing trivia to real knowing.

You can treasure hunt the language all across Britain from Avon (*afon*/river) as in Stratford-upon-Avon and Dover (*dŵr*/water) to Penrith (head of the ford). Welsh is a language that pre-dates Christianity yet exists in the age of digital technology. New words have been launched into orbit, *lloeren* for satellite, much as words such as corgi – a Welsh word meaning a small dog – have walked into the English language, along with eisteddfod and possibly penguin. But you can also get it wrong. *Moron* is Welsh for carrot; *crap* means a little knowledge; *mad* is good.

Half a million speakers may not seem a lot, but we are half way to becoming more. Over a third of the youth of Wales today are able to use the language, if they so wish. It is in them that a new dawn (meaning gift in Welsh) lies.

Let us welcome the day when the exuberance of the Welsh language depends not on the native speakers but on the rising mass of Welsh learners. Let them change the map of the language, unravel its nuances and turns, and mutations, and give this old tongue of Britain a language newly made.

Once, the Welsh language was seen as *rhad* (cheap), so cheap you could do without it. Today, it is more meaningful to say that it is *rhad ac am ddim* – not merely cheap but free – boasting a new generosity to future generations.

Menna Elfyn

The Eisteddfod

Eisteddfod is a word derived from *eistedd* – to sit. But sitting is the last thing many do at an eisteddfod, except when worn out with dancing, singing, reciting or acting. And though the National Eisteddfod towers over the smaller *eisteddfodau* we cannot diminish the impact of the annual Llangollen International Eisteddfod set up in the post war years in order to embrace a multicultural world. So too the Urdd Eisteddfod is an arena for talented young.

The eisteddfod is somewhat of a universal mystery. Almost like the Bermuda Triangle, but circular. The Welsh have always walked in circles. Only now they are doing it with conviction, with ardour, around a green and yellow pavilion that is both Taj Mahal and Lourdes magnified to immense proportions. For this piece of canvas houses Art. For one week of every year, Wales chooses its own monarchy. Based on poetic ability. We lead fellow countrymen (sic!) to the throne, present them with chairs and crowns and bow down at their feet. It is both majestic and celestial because we have made it so. It is a state of mind.

Every August, a different town provides the location for the national festival, which alternates between north and south Wales. Before the local people know it (notwithstanding spells of fund-raising and choir-making), it has sprung up in their fields as if from the pages of a pop-up book, bringing with it an elaborate congregation, marching in their green, blue and white, more often than not bringing with them the worst case of torrential rain that you've ever seen. Which is tolerable for the elder variety of eisteddfod-goers in their centrally-heated caravans and hotels but daunting for the younger members, huddled in a cold three-berth tent with only one Pot Noodle to go round. Mother Nature and the eisteddfod are sworn enemies.

However, the eisteddfod is the landmark of our survival. It is one of the oldest Welsh traditions which has developed throughout the centuries, moving from tavern to palace or castle to the seventy acres of land that it now inhabits every year. It is the cultural highlight of the year, in which Welsh literature – be it prose, free verse or the meticulous strict verse of *cynghanedd* – is prized above all. The eisteddfod is an opportunity to revel in the achievement of artists. And Welsh culture never seems to age or lack form.

The eisteddfod is also about competition, the hidden

force behind the success. Competition is about mothers and hairbrushes. It can also be about confidence and drive. The competitions spur something in the Welsh that is silent for the rest of the year. It awakens the desire to create and recreate visions of the nation as never seen before. Either through the pen, the voice, the hand, foot or paint brush.

The eisteddfod is about love and belief.

To remember is the eisteddfod's rationale for visitors from overseas, novices or veterans. To remember the Super Furry Animals bringing their peace tank onto the eisteddfod field. To remember the chain of human hands encircling the pavilion in memory of Hiroshima. To remember being poked by an umbrella for holding a placard in protest at the Prince of Wales appearing at his first (or was it his last) eisteddfod.

It is full of extravaganza, excesses and exhaustion, all through the medium of Welsh. Milkman or merchant banker, the eisteddfod has no class system. Just pure class.

Eisteddfodau are still a part of Welsh life. And at one time, every village had its own little eisteddfod which lasted well into the small hours. It was a well-known fact that competition could be vicious at many of these events. You could win at the National but not reach the last three at the Rhydlewis Eisteddfod. And if you were to absent yourself from being present on winning – it could cost you dearly. A winning poet once complained by letter that he had not received his two guinea prize, only to receive the curt reply that two guineas was also the entrance fee for the day. And since the secretary had to reply to him personally, by letter, the winner did indeed owe the eisteddfod the sum of a second-class stamp. Winners never take all at *eisteddfodau*.

How good it is that poems are priceless and poets be reminded that they are only mortals.

Menna Elfyn

'The close-ranked faces rise
With their watching, eager eyes...'
'At the Eisteddfod', Sir Lewis Morris

CASTLE
JUBILEE
SENIOR EMPRESS
SUPR
CHARITY

HOTEL
MIDLAND
SUPREME
NORTH WALES

Walls of sound, Caernarfon Castle *(above)*

Carnival queen, Ruthin *(previous page)*

A Falstaffian night, Bryn Terfel

The Steps

In front of the museum
too expensive now for Cardiffians
where John Tripp hid
his bicycle clips among the pillars
and the statue of Lloyd George
greens slowly in the drizzle
I saw Tom Jones once
eluding fans among the bushes.

Heart of the Welsh universe
its white portland replicated
perfectly in India
where the architect made a quick
rupee reselling his plans.

The past concentrates on these slabs.
Memory of marches, meetings, passions,
hired coaches like cream river-boats
the steps cut like a ghat on the Ganges.
When the sea rises
the tide will reach here with ease.

Peter Finch

Hanging around *(above)*

Art attack *(right)*

Waiter and wall flowers *(previous page)*

Rugby revelry *(above)*

A scrum of faces *(right)*

Beach bums *(above)*

Littoral explorers *(right)*

Happy hours *(above)*

Down at the (bio-dynamic) farm *(left)*

'Terrorist Ballet Dancers from Hell'

Tending dramatically towards a culture

'Things tend towards a culture', concluded the historian G.M. Young. In Wales we did not have to be told this. When, in the eighteenth century, agricultural labourers accepted jobs in the new works at Merthyr, we knew that things were already tending towards those great religious services, singing festivals, *eisteddfodau* and celebrity concerts that came to constitute our culture. From the outset there were printers preparing small white posters with plain black lettering which confirmed, from front-room windows, that we were a cultured people, albeit in an amateur way.

There were new, more garish posters to announce the week's movies. We were prepared to abandon the old faith as long as Hollywood could satisfy our dreams. The movies were totally satisfying but came gift-wrapped by other hands. Very few of our number actually visited the dream factory. 'A decade ago', said Richard Burton, 'I would have been a preacher.' So would many who went on to become not superstars but schoolteachers. We loved facts and Sunday school had taught us to enunciate clearly. Later, this stylish, confident pedantry made us natural broadcasters. As this century ends, the realisation dawns, that culture itself is a profitable commodity. Why had we been so slow to realise the true nature of our talent? Why had we sweated and groaned in field and pit when all the time we could have been in groups, broadcasting and, above all, acting and filming?

'History is not a pantomime', claimed Dennis Hay, 'and seldom, if ever, deals in sudden acts of transformation.' Clearly he had not experienced our Wales. For one moment we were all in chapel or pledging solidarity with the miners and the next wondering which of our favourite Welsh film directors would secure £1 million backing from some international corporation. Overnight *Grapes of Wrath* had been replaced by *The Last Tycoon* as a central Welsh text.

The new dawn had begun gently. A local shop-owner and old friend began to invite me to plays he was directing at various Swansea venues. The *Evening Post* had become less dominated by court cases. More space was needed for reports of young actors from west Glamorgan currently appearing in London's West End and local students successfully obtaining backing for film projects. Parents would report, anxiously at first, proudly later, that in their children's A-level work, Arts or Science were being eclipsed by Drama. Why had we wasted so many hours on Geography? *The Guardian* had suddenly become the indispensable guide to exciting new productions in small Welsh towns. Historian, Gwyn A. Williams saw his work taken up by dramatists and given a sharper edge and a new audience. Gwyn Alf's Merthyr had passed safely into the hands of Alan Osborne. We had learnt to transform the past, not merely to record it.

One of the best plugs I have seen for Swansea's Volcano Theatre was in a local Hong Kong newspaper. Banners and posters in Barcelona, Bologna, Helsinki and Edinburgh were suddenly announcing that Welsh artists, actors or film directors were in town. In London we could see plays by Peter Gill, Ed Thomas and Simon Harris, go on to Joe Allen's to dine and to argue about the state of Welsh drama. To be Welsh now was to glory in the way that Des Barrett and Daniel Evans had camped up Pyramus and Thisbe in Valleys-style, giving the Barbican one of its funniest memories.

Cardiff was once famous for rugby internationals but those matches were a mere pretext for Ed Thomas' *Songs from a Forgotten City* that records that moment when the Welsh saw through themselves. Ever since Gwyn Thomas we knew that we were all clients of an American culture, but it was Ed's *House of America* that stopped us in our tracks – suggesting it was too late for us to play at being Marlon Brando. Many London critics thought that we were trying to be Tarantinos. Certainly we remained susceptible to style. Not only did most locals accept Kevin Allen's *Twin Town* as Swansea realism but there was a sudden demand for funerals in which ashes were scattered at sea as a male voice choir sang at the end of Mumbles pier. Tarantino had taught us to look at ourselves (one school of thought even suggested his folks had a 'caff' in Aberdare). When you tend towards a culture you sway, you rock, you beg, borrow or steal, you stumble and pick up the odd £1 million cheque. That's what it's all about.

Peter Stead

Celebrating the word

Hay-on-Wye is a tiny market town at the foot of the Black Mountains of the Welsh Marches. It has thirteen hundred people and thirty-six bookshops. Once a year, for the Whitsun Bank Holiday, the town throws a party. Forty thousand people flock in from all over the world for *The Sunday Times* Hay Festival. For ten days readers, writers and musicians and comedians gather together in a carnival celebration of the word.

In the 'seventies, Richard Booth, the bookseller who started the second-hand and antiquarian business in the town, crowned himself King, and declared independence for Hay. Today the joke still entertains visitors with a certain truth. Hay is a border town, which is both Welsh and English. Hay is where Salman Rushdie made his first public appearance after the fatwa, where William Golding and Laurie Lee spoke to an audience for the last time, where the media found Bryn Terfel and Eddie Izzard, where R.S. Thomas outsells Jackie Collins, where you can meet the writers who've changed your mind.

The town is also famously inaccessible. An American bibliophile rang from an hotel in Knightsbridge: 'I can't find Hay on my map' – 'What sort of a map are you using, sir?' – 'An Underground map' – 'But, sir, we're not on the Underground, we're in Wales' – 'Geez, tell me where your nearest tube station is, will ya?' The guy arrived by cab from Heathrow. Arthur Miller didn't recognise the name of the town either – he puzzled over my telephoned invitation, and asked: 'Hay-on-Wye… is that some kind of a sandwich?' He came to see for himself, and started the pilgrimage to the town of books that brings Nobel prize winners, literary debutants and book lovers of all persuasions to the festival.

Mario Vargas Llosa, the South American novelist and sometime presidential candidate, was booked in to the festival to rhapsodise Flaubert's *Madame Bovary* on Bank Holiday Monday. He called on the Friday from Madrid. It was quite impossible for him to come. However, a flight via Heathrow and a friendly helicopter for an eight-hour round trip with twelve minutes' grace ensured his seventy minutes on stage. As he landed on the cricket field at Hay he stepped out of the chopper and beamed at the TV cameras, immortalising the town and its welcome with 'In Peru I campaigned for Head of State and they gave me a limousine, I come to Hay as a writer and they give me a helicopter.'

Peter Florence

A touch of Hay fever

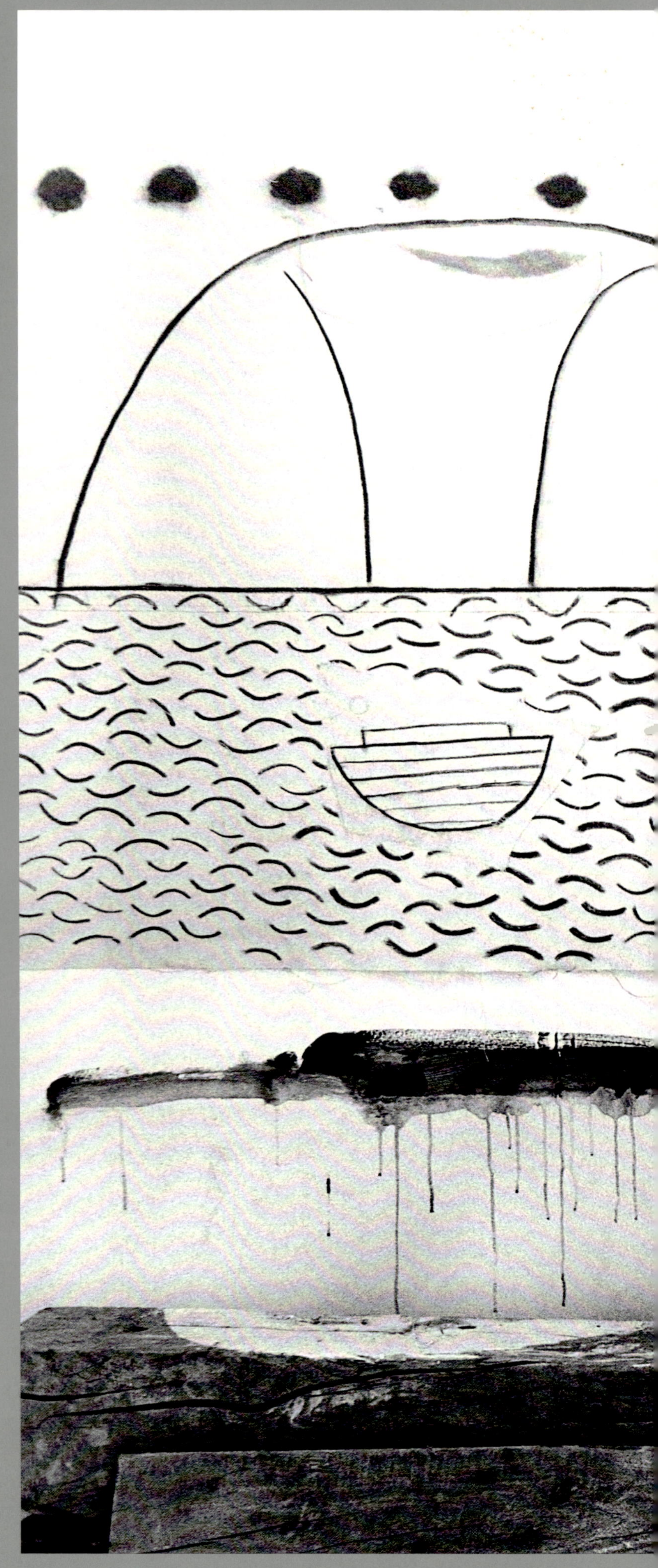

Iwan Bala, artist

BALA 97

The spectacle of seabirds at Welsh colonies rivals that of African big game; Grassholm is the world's second largest gannet colony *(above)*

Sea-horses *(left)*

Organic by design *(top)*

Blue cool *(above)*

Salmon putchers (fishing baskets) – Severn estuary *(right)*

The Unsung Park
for Gerald Morgan

Sunday morning. We younger men
come to fight for a watery egg
where the letter H is rooted twice.
We drift spasmodically between
the gates of Heaven and Hell.

My touch-judge on the edge of speech
watches the first leaf of autumn fall.
It dives for the line. He picks it up,
waves it like a warning flag.

A blue day unravels its gauze.
Heavily hung-over trees applaud
the face pressed to the wet grass.

Small worshipper, take my shirt.
We are both of us playing for time.
Your mother crosses herself on the path.
Growing too old for this game, I am
running towards the unplucked tongues
of a nation, the unmissed conversion.
Soon it is only a question of who
will perceive, (on catching the winter sun
through my bones), the scrawl of an empty nest,

eggs flown between the uprights.

Paul Henry

After snowfall

On Strumble Head

Faces of a devolution *(above)*

Arthur's hardware, Taffs Well *(right)*

KNIFE
SHARP

Designs for living

Eco-house at Penrhos *(above)*

Eco-house at Brithdir Mawr *(right)*

Evidence of early Christianity – the witness box, St. Govan's chapel *(above)*

'Architecture is frozen music' – Scott Harbour sonata *(left)*

There are places in Wales I go

In 'Reservoirs', R.S. Thomas describes places in Wales that symbolise the destruction of Welsh culture, and places he doesn't go. I was moved by the poem's dark sentiments, but it suggested to me an opposite, lighter view. I felt that there were places in Wales that had helped me focus my own views of Welsh culture and architecture – places that give me pleasure, places I go.

Portmeirion

...'All sorts of queer things,
Things never seen or heard or written about,
Very strange, un-Welsh, utterly peculiar
Things. Oh, solid enough they seemed to touch,
Had anyone dared it. Marvellous creation,
All various shapes and sizes, and no sizes,
All new, each perfectly unlike his neighbour,
Though all came moving slowly out together.'
'Welsh Incident', Robert Graves

The last thing you could imagine fitting into the rugged Welsh landscape is this tiny Italianate village. Yet how sweetly it does. Built by Wales' greatest architect of the 20th century, Clough Williams-Ellis, it is a stunning and original work of art. A pot-pourri of styles, old buildings, new ones, cupolas, collonades, steeples, balconies, terraces and monuments. It looks haphazard, a little higgledy-piggledy, but not so; it is very carefully and artfully composed. Its sugared almond colours, borrowed from the Italian seaside town of Portofino, seem odd under the grey skies of north Wales but offer a constant pleasure. It may seem trivial or purposeless but how can anyone resist its winning charm?

Pentre Ifan and House at Druidstone

... Looking for something else, I came once ...
The capstone,
Set like a cauldron on three legs,
Was marooned by the swimming crop.
A gust and the cromlech floated,
Motionless at time's moorings.
'Ancient Monuments', John Ormond

They sing a duet across Pembrokeshire, the cromlech at Pentre Ifan and the House at Druidstone. Thousands of years separate their creation but they share similar aspirations. Both are designed to be half buried, to snuggle and lodge into the landscape, yet each has its own particular presence. The grass no longer covers the great capstone of Pentre Ifan so we can now fully appreciate the brilliance of the technology. This is a delicate balancing act. We are astonished by the poise with which the colossal stone barely touches its three supports. Buried underground, the Druidstone house too revels in its technology. It looks as if the land has opened up like an eyelid to expose a huge Cyclopean window which gazes towards Ireland. This is a place dedicated to the pleasures of contemplation and recreation.

Gregynog

... Such is the strength of Art rough things to shape,
And of rude commons rich Enclosures make.
'Upon Dr Davies's British Grammar',
James Howell

From a distance it looks like any of the other black-and-white, half-timbered buildings on the Welsh border, yet it is not made of timber at all. It's all concrete! Now a university study centre, the house's greatest moments were when it was owned by the Davies sisters. They ran Gregynog as a cultural centre and their collection of impressionist art, now in the National Museum in Cardiff, once decorated these walls. Paintings by Degas, Renoir and Monet jostled for space with sculptures by Rodin. Then this was new art, vivid and shocking, vibrant in this curious building.

Carreg Cennen

... Our kings died, or they were slain
By the old treachery at the ford.
Our bards perished, driven from the halls
Of nobles by the thorn and bramble.
'Welsh History', R.S. Thomas

Rose Macaulay referred to 'the pleasure of ruins' and she was right. Ghosts can people the battlements and the dining halls. The minstrel galleries and bedchambers may be decorated in your own mind with images culled from Hollywood. Clambering through these half ruins and tunnels, the romantic feelings you first harboured are replaced by impressions of defeat and oppression. Thoughts of betrayed heroes of Welsh history, Glyndŵr and Llywelyn are only lightened by glimpses through the window openings of the vertiginous drop to the trees below or the distant ranges of the Black Mountain.

Artificial Sky, Cardiff University

I entered it before I understood it,
Knew it before I knew about it. Like smoke
The light ingathered round me ...
'Gwanwyn Nant Dywelan', Bobi Jones
(translation Joseph P. Clancy)

Architecture is not just a built environment. In the place I work we build skies in small rooms. In a blackened laboratory the lattice of a geodesic dome supports clusters of light fittings that simulate sun and cloudy sky conditions. Here we test scale models of proposed new buildings to see what the lighting conditions would be like – inside and out. Here we can produce lighting conditions that prevail anywhere in the world, at anytime of the day or year. This is a place to measure and investigate, speculate and innovate – a place for clarity and a place for dreams.

C. Malcolm Parry

'... all came moving slowly out together' – Portmeirion

'... the capstone set like a cauldron on three legs' – Pentre Ifan *(top)*

'... the land opening up like an eyelid' – House at Druidstone *(above)*

The dance of time *(above)*

The night before the morning after *(right)*

Carreg Cennen castle *(previous page)*

JVC

On the waterfront *(left)*

Copper and Slate *(following page)*

The Hedge

With hindsight, of course, I can see that the hedge
was never my cleverest idea
and that bottles of vodka are better not wedged

like fruit in its branches, to counter the fears
and the shakes in the morning on the way to work.
Looking back, I can see how I pushed it too far

when I'd stop in the lay-by for a little lurk
before plunging my torso in, shoulder high
to the hedgerow's merciful root-and-branch murk

till I'd felt out my flattie and could drink in the dry
and regain my composure with the cuckoo-spit.
Then, with growing wonder, I'd watch the fungi,

lovely as coral in the aqueous light.
Lovely, that is, till that terrible day
when the hedge was empty. Weakened by fright

I leant in much deeper to feel out which way
the bottle had rolled and, cursing my luck
(and hearing already what my bosses would say

about my being caught in this rural ruck),
I started to panic, so I tussled and heaved
and tried to stand upright, but found I was stuck.

I struggled still harder, but you'd scarcely believe
the strength in a hedge that has set its mind
on holding a person in its vice of leaves

and this one was proving a real bind.
With a massive effort, I took the full strain
and tore up the hedgerow, which I flicked up behind

me, heavy and formal as a wedding train.
I turned and saw, to my embarrassment,
that I'd pulled up a county with my new-found mane,

which was still round my shoulders, with its tell-tale scent
of loam and detritus, while trunk roads and streams
hung off me like ribbons. It felt magnificent:

minerals hidden in unworked seams
shone like slub silver in my churned-up trail.
I had brooches of newly built housing schemes

and sequins of coruscating shale;
power-lines crackled as they changed their course
and woodsmoke covered my face like a veil.

Only then did I feel the first pangs of remorse.
Still, nobody'd noticed so, quickly, I knelt,
took hold of the landscape, folded and forced

it up to a chignon which I tied with my belt.
It stayed there, precarious. The occasional spray
of blackthorn worked loose, but I quickly rebuilt

the ropey construction and tucked it away.
Since then I've become quite hard to approach:
I chew mints to cover the smell of decay

which is with me always. Food tastes of beech
and I find that I have to concentrate
on just holding the hairstyle since it's started to itch

and the people inside it are restless of late.
Still, my tresses have won me a kind of renown
for flair and I find my hair titillates

certain men who want me to take it down
in front of them, slowly. But with deepening dread
I'm watching my old self being overgrown

while scruples rustle like quadrupeds,
stoat-eyed, sharp-toothed in my tangled roots
(it's so hard to be human with a hedge on your head!).

Watch me. Any day I'll be bearing fruit,
sweet hips that glint like pinpricks of blood
and my dry land drowning will look quite cute

to those who've have never fallen foul of wood.
But on bad days now I see nothing but hedge,
my world crazed by the branches of should,

for I've lost all centre, have become an edge
and though I wear my pearls like dew
I feel that I've paid for my sacrilege

as I wish for my autumn with its broader view.
But for now I submit. With me it will die,
this narrowness, this slowly closing eye.

Gwyneth Lewis

M 49 Avonmouth
22

Ribbons of light – Severn Bridge *(above)*

To the lighthouse – South Stack, Anglesey *(left)*

A patchwork quilt covers the land – brackeny browns, silver-green sitkas, a whitening of moor grass, a delight to the eye *(above)*

Manic Street Preacher – James Dean Bradfield *(right)*

Mending the mountain path – Snowdonia *(previous page)*

'You shall see gamesters return home
from this play with broken heads,
black faces, bruised bodies and
lame legs, yet laughing and merrily
jesting at their harms...'
George Owen of Henllys 1603

The Crowd

Sport is the only Welsh Dream which has fixed points in the calendar and thousands fretfully waking for Match Day. Anticipation butterflied in the stomach to the point of anxiety. An International. A League Decider. A Cup Final.

The same routine of fingered tickets, excited phone calls and the fast-forward projector of the mind which has your team, through the pulse and flow of frantic minutes, claim the prize. And if it truly happens that way then the re-wind button will allow last year's imagery to flicker behind your eyes as you join the people always rushing through the streets to become the Crowd.

The beauty of the Crowd is that it is never anonymous. As you congregate you do so in knots, in couples, in groups, in discovery. From the enclosure the play is framed by the familiar: hunched-shouldered hills with buckled terraces clinging on for the ride, rivers silently sliding past behind the Grandstand and the punctuating motion of indifferent trains on lines parallel to this momentarily more real world.

The Crowd is generational, shades flit through it, accepting they have been jostled out of their chosen viewing places but there, blessing us for our continued presence, all the same. We are sharers in the passion. Our five living senses still connecting to that evanescence of Memory which is the real stuff of life. History in the present moment.

We hear and remember the particular smack or thud or stroke of the ball, decade by decade, player by player, leather on leather, hide on plastic, in the wet or from the dust. We see faces lined by exertion beyond bodily sense, mad with wonder, puffed in achievement. We touch each other in our eagerness to participate in the goal scored, the ball fumbled, the penalty taken, the catch dropped by our significant, better, other, selves, the run sublime made. We smell the seasons' turning in the air and sense how teams move to different rhythms. We taste the unbidden desire on our tongues, the arid mouth, the bilious surge, the sweet, sweet victory which will now, never, soon come.

Only an urban society could bring all this to the Welsh. Iron, coal and steel and slate and tinplate and railways and docks, made our cities, towns and industrial valleys the receptacles for spectator sport and in their kitchen cauldrons we alchemised golden heroes from common clay for modern Wales.

We have no need of Myths now.

What was common has become collectively possessed through the very individuality of these heroes. Invidious to name them. They crossed the Atlantic to tantalise with a dancing skill learned on the scuffed canvases of tawdry halls or rose, senselessly majestic in the air, to alter the geometry of still netting. We re-create them, in all their sports and at many levels, because we can no longer live without them.

Of course the collective pride is irrational. When that hurdler swoops through the tape and is wrapped in the red dragon flag the incredible triumph is not the nation's but yet the winner bears the nation within. We are the flag which covers the runner. We are the banner carried into the ring, taken to the ground, kissed as the medal circles the neck.

Yet such identity through sport is universal now. It is a global identikit displacement of the complex in favour of the measurable moment, nationality brought to a generous point. Such identity through sport transfixes us because it is rooted, differentially, in separate histories.

This is ours, we want to say. It moves on and is no more a simple progress than life itself. But follow it with us, its present and its past, and you will trace the lineaments of the modern Welsh more clearly in its cries and echoes than in anything else.

Dai Smith

Field glasses, Chepstow

Benthic warrior – Menai Straits *(above)*

Doing the rounds – cheesemaking at Cenarth *(right)*

Bayside statuary

Swinging town – Brecon Jazz Festival

Frozen Tarn

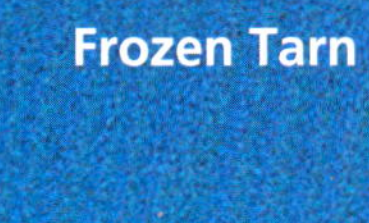

Some queen has left her mirror on the grass.
If I could pick it up the back
would be metal, the chased whorl and counter-whorl,
all the mystic twisting.

She's left it tilted, reflecting
the dark fringe of trees
and the grey huddle of hills.
Her mirror holds the only empty spaces.

One of those women from the ancient tales
– the tragic, defiant ones –
always with a witty answer on their tongues
and usually some secret in a tower room.

A cold oval of myth on the winter hillside,
and you, far down there
bending over, stepping out on her polished treachery,
balanced on a moving iron cloud.

Catherine Fisher

Faces at the market – Abergavenny

'The mountain sheep are sweeter ...'

Like the poor they're always with us, as unavoidable as the weather and as inescapably part of our landscape and psyche as castles, daffodils or leeks. You will find them searching a bin-bag for a stale bun or a banana as joyfully as they chew moor-grass or blueberries on their native crags, for like the urban fox they have reached their own accommodation with the times.

Snowdonia is the ancestral home of our original mountain stock, small, artful, wiry and devious. Unlike more refined breeds, they have long bristly hairs, kemp, red or white, the bane of the knitting and weaving trades, which sheds the heaviest rain and breaks the wildest wind. They wear their wool well greased with lanolin, thick and close to the skin. It is a haven for mites, ticks and lice, as any shepherd will tell you, but as warm as any spacesuit or gas oven.

Notoriously difficult to contain within their boundary fence, they have spread south across Pumlumon and the Cambrian Mountains, over the Brecon Beacons and down the valleys of the coalfield – and westwards, for you can see the hardy Welsh happy on the tip of Llŷn and skipping amongst the rocks of Gower.

They are hated by gardeners and conservationists for gobbling every flower that blooms, they are the despair of economists and marketing men for being so anarchic and unpredictable, and they are dismissed from conventional English dinner tables as only fit for the Celts and Italians. Agriculturally as marginal as the barren uplands from which they come, they survive and multiply by scavenging what they can and stealing when they have to. They live principally off fresh air, subsidies and tradition.

In the fertile lands of Pembroke, Gwent and the Vale of Glamorgan, over on the plains of Cheshire and in the lush meadows of Herefordshire, you can often see them crossed with broadly-built Suffolks, hard-nosed Wiltshires or superior Leicesters. More recently there has been much inter-breeding with all sorts of continentals – the Charolais, Texels and Bleu de Maine.

It is hard to get the Welsh to fit into the standard specification necessary to stuff the polystyrene containers on the supermarket shelf, for they are plagued by nonconformity and individualism. In fact, those who know about these things have a word for them, and they don't mean it kindly – Welsh, they call them, Welsh.

Patrick Dobbs

Bog snorkelling – Llanwrtyd Wells *(above)*

In proportion – Snowdon from the Pyg track *(right)*

Rave on

BETHLEHEM

A day at the races

The publishers thank HSBC, Hyder, Laing, S4C and the WDA for their support and their commitment to this publication. Thanks are extended to the photographers and writers for their contribution to this collaborative work as well as to Alan Padbury/The Westdale Press, Stephen Shaw/Design Principle and Ian Davies/Bay Graphics for their supreme efforts.

The publishers also thank Robert Horne and Idéal, Peter Finch/Yr Academi Gymraeg, Neil Fowler and Tim Dickeson/Western Mail, Tony Bianchi/Cyngor Celfyddydau Cymru (The Arts Council of Wales), Mairwen Prys Jones/Gwasg Gomer, Iestyn Hughes/National Library of Wales, Mike Thomas/Colab and Dyfed Elis-Gruffydd for their support and advice along the way. This gratitude is extended to the many others (too numerous to mention) whose encouragement has been both sustained and sustaining. Diolch yn fawr.

Complete poems re-printed with kind permission of authors and publishers as follows: Hilary Llewellyn-Williams 'Deep Song' from *Animaculture* (Seren), © Hilary Llewellyn-Williams; Herbert Williams 'The Aliens' from *Ghost Country* (Gomer), © Herbert Williams; Oliver Reynolds 'Bestiary' from 'Tone Poem' from *The Player Queen's Wife* (Faber & Faber), © Oliver Reynolds; Peter Finch 'The Steps' from *Useful* (Seren), © Peter Finch; Paul Henry 'The Unsung Park' from *Captive Audience* (Seren), © Paul Henry; Gwyneth Lewis 'The Hedge' from *Parables and Faxes* (Bloodaxe 1995), © Gwyneth Lewis; Mike Jenkins 'Promising Light' (for Al Jones, photographer), © Mike Jenkins.

Short extracts used in *'There are places I go'* by C. Malcolm Parry have been taken from the following: 'Welsh Incident' by Robert Graves (*Collected Poems*, 1965); 'Ancient Monuments' by John Ormond (*Definition of a Waterfall*, 1973); 'Gwanwyn Nant Dywelan' gan Bobi Jones (*Y Gân Gyntaf*, 1957) translation by Joseph P. Clancy; 'Welsh History' by R.S. Thomas; 'Upon Dr. Davies's British Grammar' by James Howell.

Every effort has been made to trace copyright owners. The publishers would like to apologise for any inadvertent errors or omissions from the above.

Index of photographers and writers

Claiming the future